T0368484

AuthorHouse™
1663 Liberty Drive
Bloomington, IN 47403
www.authorhouse.com
Phone: 1 (800) 839-8640

Published by AuthorHouse 5/19/2015

ISBN: 978-1-5049-0301-1 (sc)
978-1-5049-0303-5 (hc)
978-1-5049-0302-8 (e)

Library of Congress Control Number: 2015905109

Print information available on the last page.

Any people depicted in stock imagery provided by Thinkstock are models,
and such images are being used for illustrative purposes only.
Certain stock imagery © Thinkstock.

This book is printed on acid-free paper.

authorHOUSE®

Garden of Love

Growing Vegetables, Children and Inspirations

Amanda Hansen

Welcome to my vegetable garden. All different plants you will see,

From, salad fixings, to salsa
makings, to eggplants and
some flowers for bees.

My vegetable garden has a name, it's called "The Garden of Love" and rightfully its name is what it became...

"What do you mean? Said the boy in blue, How could a garden become its name?!"
"Come with me" said the gardener "Let me tell you"

This garden took much
of my patience and
much of my work.
She said with a smirk.

"The dirt had many weeds and I had to pull all of them before I planted my seeds.

My eggplant didn't grow
when I thought it would,
but that squash you see,
I had more than I
thought I could"

My spinach grew very fast
and the lettuce seemed
to come in... slow

Those red peppers by
the tomatoes, I thought
they would never grow.

My patience was especially testing me when bugs started eating my plants and my bum was getting bit by many ants!

All those weeds I pulled,
came back over night. I spent
many days pulling them, with
no growing vegetables in sight

The wind blew the flower
petals right off and all
the cotton in the air
gave me a cough."

"So how does that make it
"The garden of love?""
said the boy in blue.
The gardener smiled
and said "Just wait, I'm
not done telling you.

All that work I put into
my garden, I did with a
smile and with that smile
my garden produced
vegetables worthwhile!

I never gave up and
I didn't doubt
With hard work my lettuce
would finally sprout.

My zucchini didn't just
feed me; it fed my
friends and family too

And with a little extra water my pumpkins grew bigger then you.

On one really sunny day, my whole garden tripled in size.

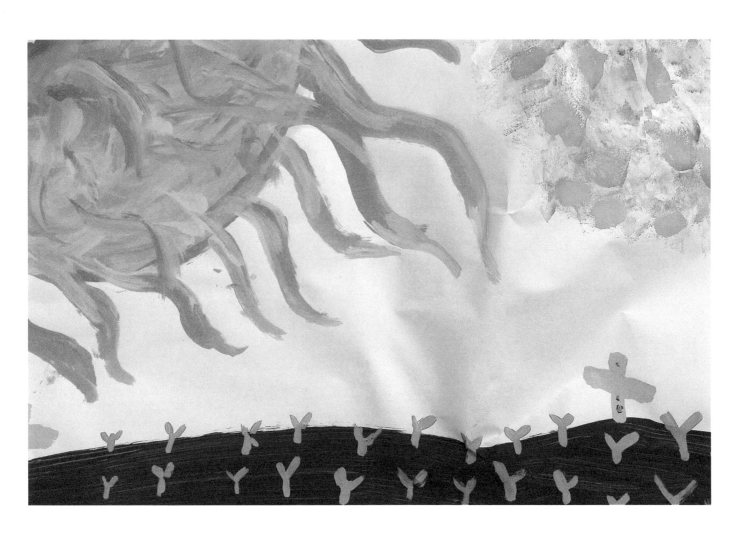

This garden took work and
caught me by surprise.

I can never give up on
this vegetable garden
just like how I can never
give up on love.

Always, with hard work
and patience you will grow
something to be proud of.

Love can hurt, just
like pulling weeds.

But nothing will ever
grow if you don't plant
and water the seeds.

"I understand now"
said the boy in blue.

You showed the garden
love and the garden did
the same for you."

"Yes, "The Garden of
Love" is what grew."

Printed in the United States
By Bookmasters